All the Wrong Places

Abbey Lynne Rays

Presentation by *BookLeaf Publishing*

Web: www.bookleafpub.com

E-mail: info@bookleafpub.com

ISBN: 978-93-95271-70-7

First edition 2022

For the women who, like me,

take a little longer

finding their "happy ever after."

ACKNOWLEDGEMENT

Grateful acknowledgement is made to Querencia Press, which originally printed the following poems in their anthology: "Still I Hope" and "Hiding From You at the First Street Ale House"

Thank you to BookLeaf Press for choosing to publish my chapbook. Seeing my words in print is truly a dream come true. Thank you for holding the Writeathon and inspiring me to sit, write, and put this whole thing together. I am forever grateful.

To my first reader, Jen Kaur. Thank you for your constant support. The way you hype up my poetry is nothing short of amazing! Thank you for reading my poetry and holding my hand through difficult times.

To the Instagram writing community who has supported and inspired me the last five years. Thank you! The strength, compassion, and talent I read daily are a constant source of inspiration and motivation.

Sharlene, I told you I would do it! Thanks for believing in me all these years!

Dad, thank you for always supporting me.

Ryan, thank you for being my biggest fan and showing me what a real partner is supposed to look like. You are everything and so worth the wait.

And lastly, thank you, dear reader, for taking the time to read my book. It took my twenty plus years to follow through on this passion project. This is only the beginning.

Cover acknowledgements:
Thank you Erica Santos for author photo and stylings
Thank you @igorkrasnoselskyi for the graphic used in the cover design

Portions of this text were previously published in another format on the author's social media.

"I suppose the years erase only what we want, days get easier, when if we choose them to be, and each moon that rises is just one more chance to create new dreams, ripe with our torn fragments, and exposed to chance again."

A.L. Rays

Hunger

You tell me that compatibility
    is a better investment than chemistry.
That the ease of washed dishes and
    bullets bitten back undeclared
are worth the glitz
    of a thousand midnight confessions.

But I say no.

I want to be touched with desire
drizzling onto stuttering flesh.
I want wildflowers and scratches
    and the passion of tin roofs and rain.
I want fire and fever burning my insides
and the past
    until I am drowning
    until I can do nothing more
 than bite your mouth in hunger
    sucking the sweetness
        from the red hot flame.

I want to be turned upside down.

You laugh at my naivety.
You tell me the real world isn't like that.
Nothing that ripe can ever last.

But I have had the other,
    I have fallen to the stars,
white-washed and unglued,
praying for cracks to explain
my utter discontent.
    Drinking hot coffee
            in a blue kitchen,
unhungry for omelets
                adventures
                kisses.
Swimming in the nothingness
    of easy breath.

Oasis Grill

Your fingers grip
Greek dolmathes
    in a tight fingered pinch
  as you talk of past women,
    and the trips to Napa
where you unfolded
their sinewy limbs
    and your heart
in the swelling ache
    their skirts spilt out.

You tell me you fell
as quickly as they left
you, in a perplexing bathos,
tell me how you felt used
    by their caution,
their absence,
their hesitation of certainty.

Rice falls
    from grape leaves
to our wooden table
    splattering as angrily
  as the memories
    in your far away eyes.

I wonder why you tell me this.
　　I sigh.
　The faint melody of understanding
　　　that desire will not
bloom here
　　in a sleepy restaurant at dusk.
Your lips are bruised and
　　your fingers clumsy.
They are constantly reaching out,
　flailing, stumbling, stuttering.
Every woman's body
　an untempered levy
you linger behind lopsided,
　unmapped territories
you cut through unhinged.
You are content
with any that might shimmer.

You Here

5

The shock of you. Here.
Between walls
where my arms
dangle carelessly.
You. Here.
A place where my
eyes narrow with cocky apathy,
where I smile
just to show my teeth,
where I laugh
because I have no words.
You. Here.
My eyes recognize
your certain outline,
my mind gathering
clues in the
 familiar landscape.
Your name falling
like a question on my
loose numb lips.

I kiss you to be certain,
and without a thought,
fall again, unplanned
into the dips of your flesh

as you smile kisses
onto my frozen cheeks.

All the Wrong Places

When you are a child
Who's mother walks out
you are left feeling
unwanted.

At 19 with
Sly smiles,
skinny cigarettes
I invited love,
a stuttering creciendo,
rash & discontented.
Swollen with hope
that these transient
flashes could finally
stitch together
some kind of proof
that I was worth
all the want
she left me yearning for.

Still I Hope

I was not naive
no, I knew
men who kiss your
fingers at night,
tilt your face to
the moon
and beg you to stay,

Often wake with
a tangle of haste.
full of realization
their heart
Not ready to leap
farther than bedsides
Dark mouths a sieve
to last nights song

A little shatter I
prepare for. I
know desire is
a messy thing.
Still, I choose
hope. Give in to
the frivolous swell
knotting and blooming

beneath my rib
and pray.

Hollywood Dreams

Don't tell me I don't take chances.
I packed up my Hyundai,
and drove myself
all the way
to L.A.

Showed up in Hollywood
with garbage bags full
of what the suitcase
could not hold.

Found a group of thespians
At TGI Fridays,
made my living room
 a stage,

mimicked blocking,
found the beats,
practiced saying
I love you.

Almost believing it.

Then I met him.
Lip twist,

eyebrow raise,
tongue thrust
I tried,
mouthing the words,

But no sound
would come.

All That is Holy

I am a gut punch.
A wet kiss,
mouth to hot mouth.
A kick of bourbon
under flickering street lights.

A manual on escape,
peeling sideways
when the mood strikes.

A blanket of honey
on a scratchy throat,
meaty enough to feed you
but then again I might not.

I'll share stories about
my mother,
locked in back rooms.
How I never knew her,
never met her dreams.

I'll let you splice open
my shadows,
cleaving the marrow
of my being

my root
to the stars and beyond,
to the dust of what is.

You will find meaning
in my scars.
Even the crescent one,
ragged and inelegant.
Trace it
with your tongue,
taste each prayer,
let it linger, stick.

Meeting You

The chemistry was palpable.
You kissed me
before you asked my name,
as if the heat of my mouth
might burn a path to the answer.
The need for ritual or normalcy
evaporated eloquently, and
eagerly on the tip of my tongue

There was no illusion of composition,
or explanations
just the scent of loneliness shaken
 with the aggression of surety,
desire swirling, flashing, pressing.

And then
bottles breaking,
spilling out months waiting,
stars and sin startling the sky
smearing possibility into the
wake of my breathe.

I was far too good for you.
We both knew it.

But the absence of speech
left all scrutinizes invisible.

 I let your kisses
pour into me, the anger
of your past.
I drank it up
biting your lips,
savoring the taste,
thick with danger,
the delight of a man
unhesitated
in each choice and
 step he takes.

Consumed

I am the type
to get consumed.
swallowed by my
own thoughts,
ravished by
poetry,
nature,
and the
thought of you.

Already Lost

Something changed
from that first night

to those that followed.
Like a spell
broken.

Your eyes did not linger
Your lips did not smile,
stupidly like a boy
wishing for more than he
should take

You asked me nothing
you told me less

and when we lay to sleep
there was comfort
but no passion

No eagerness pressed my body
no desire to unwrap me

your hand in my own
I watched you sleep

and wondered
sadly
what dreams
were already lost
and what exactly
you were still
holding tight to
when you wrapped me
in your arms.

Addiction

Sometimes
I pretended
I understood
more than I did.

Truth be told,
I do not understand
the fears you have
the pain,
the craving,
the regrets.

But I understand grief,
and I understand
the fight
to put yourself
back together again.

I understand hope.
 I understand
how it can both
inspire
and wreck a person
depending on the day,
depending on the dream.

And I understand love.
And how often
it is not nearly enough
to be what we need.

Spent

My forgiveness
    spent,
my love a sore surplus
bagged again,
by my brutal niceties,
    and broken down
by your hard simplicity.
We never were
    as we showed.

Instead of fighting
    together,
we fought each other.
Until we were stripped
    of comfort, passion,
        pain,
until we were simply
cool indifferent pools
of stillness,
    just waiting
for another perfect ripple.

Instagram Post

The smiles
in these pictures
told me
everything I
needed to know.

They were the words
you couldn't say
the conversation
you avoided.

She was more of
what you needed
and I was simply
less.

Speak

When did our voices become
    archaic tears
we shake from bed linens
    and wipe from fine china?

Must I read your weeps
    in text or emails and
feel your punctured discontent
through my own imagined syllables?
I glaze your swollen trembles
    with the trails of night
wind washed
    and tough tasting on my tongue.

I know not what to speak.

I have swallowed the sleepless
goodbye of lovers,
    silently cracking
the remembrance of desire,
    swift- soft and suffocating
without the guttural sound of truth.
    The text my love, ripped me.

I have also wept for my mother.
Tangled southern anger
        dissipating,
remembering always
      the noise that spiraled
on the creamy white skin
      of my youthful limbs,
echoing slowly,
years awakened
        after decades of silence.
The email my blood, wrecked me.

Are there things larger than speech?
Larger than the voice
      of another sturdy rainstorm?
I am rattled by the
rain biting down,
    with it's shrieking screams
          and stories
Does nothing else have faith in noise?

Or are some things too sorrowful,
      too regretful
that our ripe mouths
      are simply unable
to form the barbs,
      and shoot them caustically
where love and elegance
    once rolled and bloomed to kisses?

Who Taught You

Who taught you
that
 gentle hearts
should break without
noise?

or that
people can be
erased?
replaced?
Left weeping.
Left.
All because you
cant decide
what's worth saving,
outside the borders
of your own skin.

Gemini

I still read your horoscope
trying to figure out
the clues
that you never spoke

Trying to
unwrap your heart
and understand
if it were
the beating
or the timing
that for us
was out of sync.

Hiding From You at the Hopyard Alehouse

The last time I saw you,
I ran
   out the door,
     around the corner,
fear a tangle of thorns
   and lilac prayers.
I did not trust my eyes
    not to sing of heartbreak.
Drunk shadows swelled
   with regret and gathered
stone- like in my throat
    thundering the sweetness
with its thieving desire.

I still can't say
    if you saw me run.
If it cut your heart
   like a shard of regret
 plunging quickly
the distance of
   past and present.
If that icicle of sorrow
   polluted your Pale Ale,
unraveled your calm and

illuminated your choice
		into the expansion of solitude.
		Or if rather you sat
unaffected
			by the rippling waves of
desire and disgust,
		malleable and pressing,
and still,
		seasons later,
		stealing the air of promise.

Left in Costanoa

Have you
swept my footprints
from your heart?
Eager to dispose
of their ill measured mess?
Or did you keep them
to trace your memories around
on days the softness
has fallen from your fingers?

I think about you sometimes,
when the nights
are too warm for October.
I never know how to feel
when your face forms in my mind.
You have fallen
 from where I carried you.
Fallen from expectancies
of what I meticulously
created every one
of those beautiful days past.

I wonder
how your heart feels,
far from the beat of my own

and if regret has taken root,
seamlessly woven in memories
and shut behind solid doors.

Or if instead
you move easily
in life's continuance,
the trail of yesterday
blown away swiftly,
surely,
and with the carelessness
that still comes
with that easy
ocean breeze.

Heart I Tend To First

31

Last night I dreamt
   I saw the sorry in your eyes.
I felt the warmth
  of your open palm and
    I smiled as I unwound
   all the hurt you braided.

This morning I awoke
   where no apologies hung
 except for the many
   I feverishly whispered
to myself.
Your face just a memory
   in a quickly fading dream.

Anger

Boy, today I woke up
and was no longer sad.
Today I woke up angry.

Angry at you
for making me feel less
simply so you could
deserve more.
Angry at you
for opening a heart
you had no intention
of exploring.
Angry at you
for not knowing
which way
your heart should walk.

But as that anger heated
my shaky limbs
I realized
the truth.
I could not blame you
for risking
the same thing I did.
I could not blame you

for hoping,
even when
hope was not
 the wisest option.
And I could not blame you
for being honest
when it no longer felt right.

No, I blame myself
for staying silent
at times I should have spoke
and speaking at
times I should have listened.
I blame myself
for accepting
behavior that slowly
broke me inside,
words that cut,
actions that made me feel
like I was slowly disappearing.

I am not angry with you.

You are too broken to know
the way to a heart
or back again.
I am angry with myself
for drawing out a map
and believing that

was enough
for you to find your way.
For believing you should.
For believing I needed you to.

Epilogue

35

Do not let
these lies fool you
I still look
for glimmers of you
everywhere.

and when I sleep
your name fills my
breath
and feeds me
hope
wild and dangerous
but so worth
every taste.